EMTs

by Kristin L. Nelson

PULL AHEAD BOOKS
Community Helpers

Lerner Publications Company • Minneapolis

Lerner Publications Company
A division of Lerner Publishing Group, Inc.
241 First Avenue North
Minneapolis, MN 55401 U.S.A.

Website address: www.lernerbooks.com

Words in **bold type** are explained in a glossary on page 31.

Library of Congress Cataloging-in-Publication Data

Nelson, Kristin L.
    EMTs / by Kristin Nelson.
      p. cm. — (Pull ahead books)
    Includes index.
    ISBN: 978–0–8225–1690–3 (lib. bdg. : alk. paper)
    1. Emergency medical technicians—Juvenile literature.
  I. Title.
  RC86.5.N45 2005
  616.02'5'023–dc22   2004011627

Manufactured in the United States of America
2 – BP – 7/15/11

Look! There goes an ambulance with its lights flashing.

Where is it going?

A speedy ambulance is on its way to help someone in trouble. This is an **emergency!**

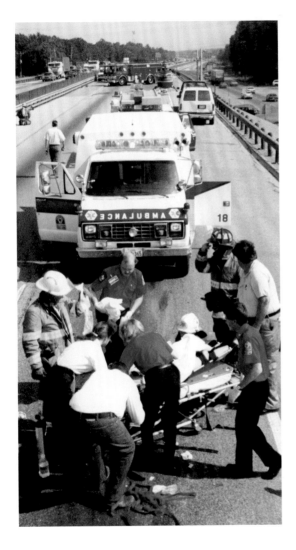

An emergency
is a problem
that needs
attention fast.

People called emergency medical
technicians hurry to the scene.
They will help!

Emergency medical technicians are also called EMTs.

EMTs do an important job. They help people in the **community** who are hurt or sick.

Your community is made up of people
in your neighborhood, town, or city.

In an emergency, EMTs go right to the person who is hurt or sick. This person is called the **patient.**

EMTs have to make decisions quickly.
They also have to stay calm when
someone is in danger.

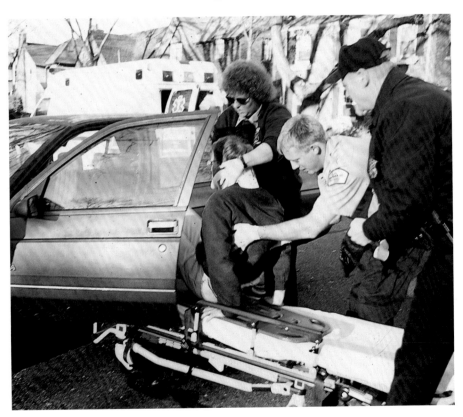

Every EMT carries a **first aid kit**.

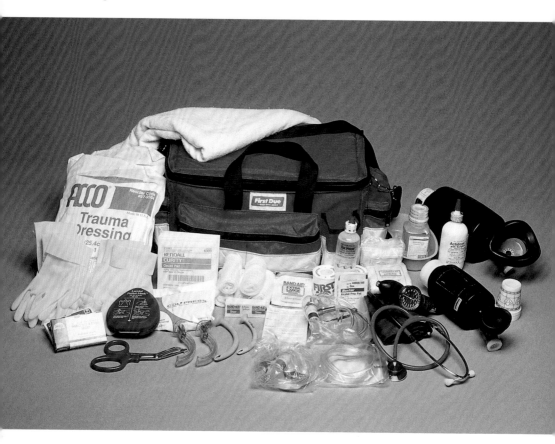

What kinds of things are in this kit?

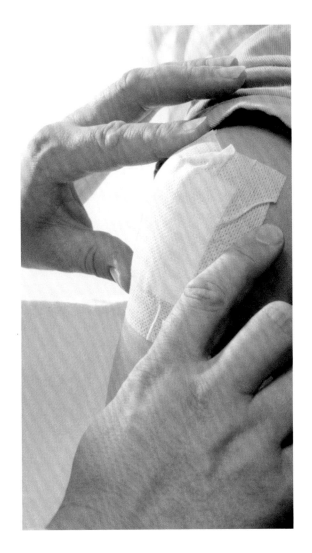

All kits have bandages. EMTs use bandages and tape to treat scrapes and cuts.

Some patients have trouble breathing. An EMT uses an **oxygen mask** to help this patient get enough air.

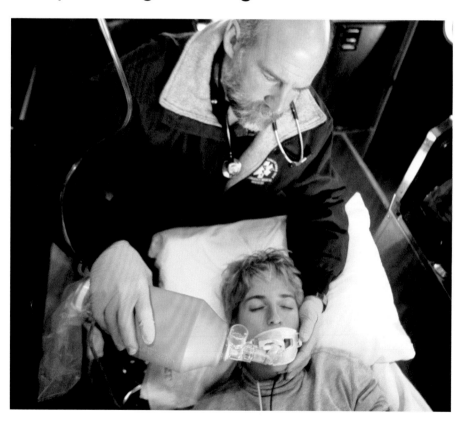

This patient has a broken arm. An EMT puts a **splint** on her arm. The splint keeps the arm from moving. The broken bone will heal faster if it stays still.

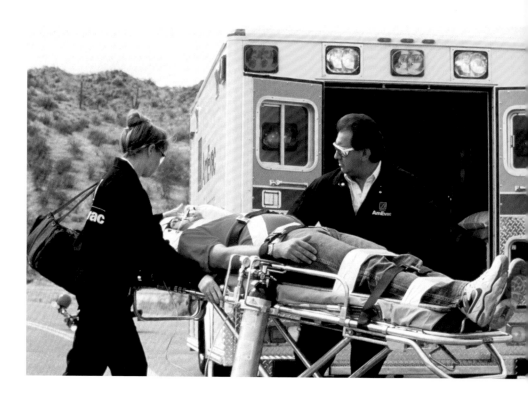

EMTs often need to take patients to the hospital for more care. They use **stretchers** to move patients. This patient is lying on a stretcher.

A stretcher is like a bed. The belts on the stretcher keep the patient safe and secure. Some stretchers have wheels.

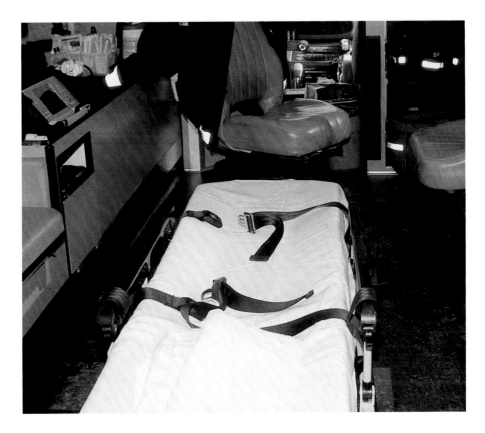

The EMTs lift the patient into the back of the ambulance. Off they go!

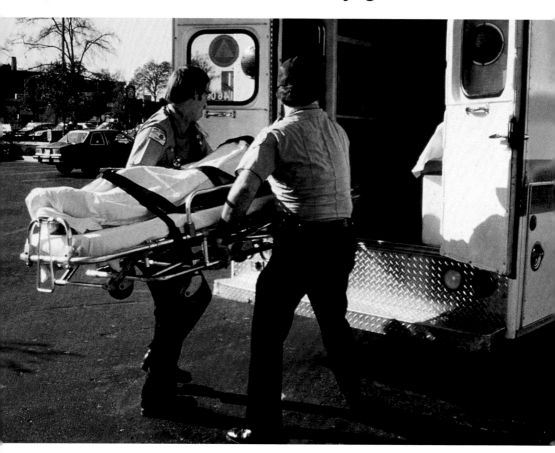

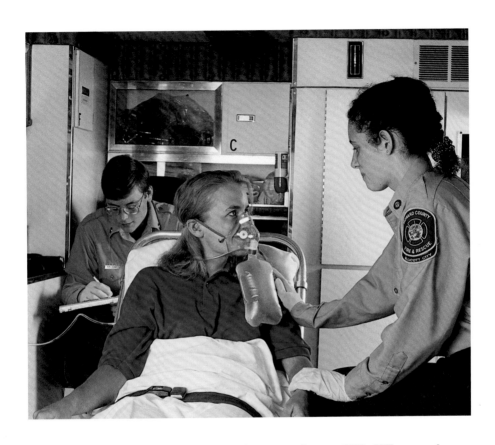

One EMT drives. The other EMTs take care of the patient. They keep her comfortable.

The ambulance arrives at the hospital.
The EMTs take the patient to the
emergency room.

At the hospital, the EMTs talk to a doctor. They share what they know about the patient's health.

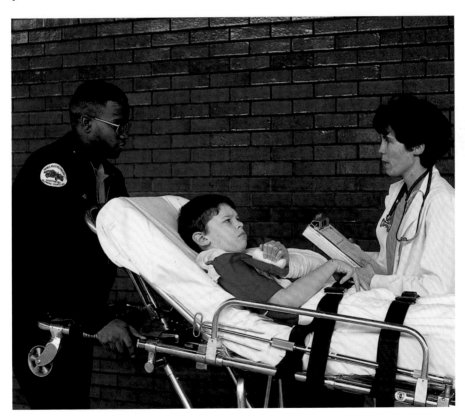

Once the patient is safe, EMTs clean
the ambulance. They make sure that it
has everything it needs.

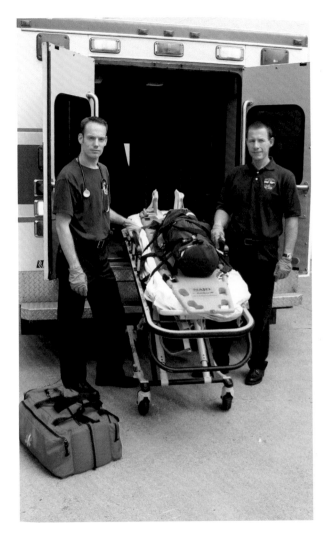

EMTs have to be ready for the next emergency!

Would you like to be an EMT someday?

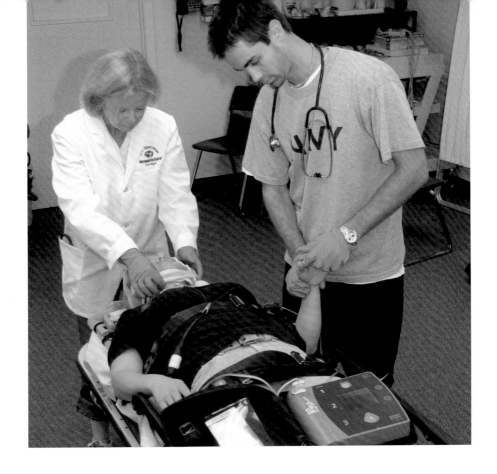

People need special **training** to become EMTs. They learn and practice new first aid skills. Then they can be EMTs.

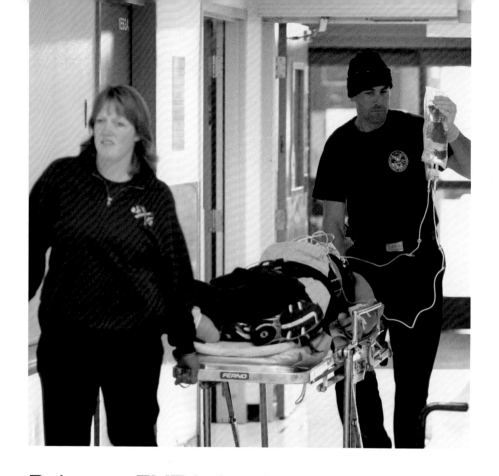

Being an EMT is hard work. EMTs
move quickly to help people. They save
lives every day.

The next time you see an ambulance with its lights flashing, remember EMTs. Think about the important job they do!

Facts about EMTs

- Did you know that there are three kinds of EMTs? An emergency medical technician can be an EMT-Basic, an EMT-Intermediate, or an EMT-Paramedic. What is the difference? Each level requires more training. A paramedic has the most training.

- EMTs work in many different places. Some work for hospitals. Others work for police or fire departments.

- Many EMTs work long hours. Some have to work evenings, weekends, and even holidays or overnight. EMTs have to be ready to help anytime there is an emergency!

EMTs through History

■ Hundreds of years ago, a person who needed medical help was placed on a chariot. A chariot is a two-wheeled cart pulled by horses. On chariots, patients lay in swinging beds called hammocks.

■ Emergency medical workers used horse-drawn ambulances for hundreds of years. In 1899, a Chicago hospital got the first ambulance with a motor in the United States. It only went 16 miles per hour.

■ In the 1950s, most hospitals did not have emergency rooms. But some hospitals set up special areas to handle emergencies. These areas were usually in the back of the building. When there was an emergency, the ambulance driver rang the hospital doorbell. A nurse unlocked the door and then called the doctor at home. The doctor came as soon as possible.

More about EMTs

Find out more about EMTs with these books and websites.

Books

Brill, Marlene Targ. *Doctors.* Minneapolis: Lerner Publications Company, 2005.

Brill, Marlene Targ. *Nurses.* Minneapolis: Lerner Publications Company, 2005.

Kottke, Jan. *A Day with Paramedics.* New York: Children's Press, 2000.

Levine, Michelle. *Ambulances.* Minneapolis: Lerner Publications Company, 2004.

Websites

Girl Power! National Emergency Services Week
http://www.girlpower.gov/girlarea/05may/EMSweek.htm

Kid Safety—How Do You Call for Help in an Emergency?
http://www.lawtonpd.com/kids/kpemerge.htm

What Happens in the Emergency Room?
http://kidshealth.org/kid/feel_better/places/er.html

Glossary

community: a group of people who live in the same city, town, or neighborhood

emergency: a problem that needs attention right away

first aid kit: a box or bag with bandages, tape, and other things to help a patient

oxygen mask: a mask that fits over a patient's mouth and brings air to his or her lungs

patient: a person who needs medical attention

splint: a stiff piece of material that keeps an injured arm or leg from moving

stretchers: tools to help move patients who are sick or injured. Many stretchers look like beds with seat belts. Some have legs and wheels. Stretchers with wheels are also called ambulance cots or gurneys.

training: information about and practice in a new skill

Index

ambulance, 3–4, 18, 19, 20, 22, 27, 29

bandages, 13
broken arm, 15

doctor, 21, 29

emergency, 4–5, 6, 10, 11, 18–19, 23, 28, 29
emergency room, 20

first aid kit, 12

history, 29
hospital, 16, 20–21, 28, 29

oxygen mask, 14

patient, 10, 14–16, 18, 19–21

splint, 15
stretcher, 16–18

training, 25, 28

Photo Acknowledgments

The photographs in this book appear courtesy of: © Todd Strand/Independent Picture Service, front cover, pp. 17, 23, 25; © Jim Baron/ The Image Finders, p. 3; © Tom McCarthy/Photo Network, p. 4; © Mary Myers/911 Pictures, p. 5; © Lawrence Porter/911 Pictures, pp. 6, 9; PhotoDisc Royalty Free by Getty Images, pp. 7, 10, 20; © Michael Heller/911 Pictures, p. 8; © Mark E. Gibson/ The Image Finders, p. 11; © Steve Agricola/Photo Network, pp. 12, 19, 21, 22; © Royalty-Free/CORBIS, p. 13; © Tom Stewart/CORBIS, pp. 14, 27; © Sam Lund/Independent Picture Service, p. 15; © Michal Heron/CORBIS, p. 16; © Novastock/Image Finders, p. 18; © MacDonald/Photo Network, p. 24; © Ed Kashi/CORBIS, p. 26; © Museum of the City of New York/Byron Collection/Getty Images, p. 29.